HEMP JEWELRY

EASY-TO-MAKE DESIGNS
FOR BOHO CHIC STYLE

SUZANNE MCNEILL

Published 2015 – IMM Lifestyle Books
www.IMMLifestyleBooks.com

IMM Lifestyle Books are distributed in the UK by Grantham Book Service.

In North America, IMM Lifestyle Books are distributed by
Fox Chapel Publishing
1970 Broad Street
East Petersburg, PA 17520
www.FoxChapelPublishing.com

ISBN 978-1-5048-0015-0

Printed in the United States of America
First printing

Bring out Your Boho Style!

Natural hemp or hemp in earthy colors goes perfectly with boho-chic or surfer-chic style. If you love this look, embellish your hemp projects with wood beads, turquoise accents, shells, or other elements that have a nature-inspired theme.

Natural elements like shells pair
wonderfully with hemp designs.

Colored hemp in muted or neutral tones like coral and navy creates an earthy vibe.

Go all out with a bag necklace inspired by Native American medicine bags.

Whether you need a casual bracelet for
your favorite t-shirt and jeans combo
or a striking necklace to pair with a
summery dress, you will find loads of
ideas in this book. Experiment with
color and embellishments to make these
designs truly your own. Have fun!

Contents

Multi-Strand Overhand
Knot Bracelet   20

Beads and Braids
Necklace   22

Simple Wrapped
Bracelet   24

Beaded Woven Bracelet   26

Two-Color
Twist Bracelet   28

Beaded Half Hitch
Bracelet   30

Shell Bracelet   30

Josephine Knot Necklace 34

Multi-Strand Josephine
Knot Bracelet   34

Beaded Josephine Knot
Bracelet   35

Simple Half Knot
Bracelet   38

Two-Color Half
Knot Bracelet   38

Bold Bead Necklace   39

Beaded Twist
Necklace   40

THE BASICS

Hemp bracelets and embroidery floss friendship bracelets are often spoken of synonymously, so why use hemp? While embroidery floss can be used for some hemp designs, and thin hemp can be used for some embroidery floss designs, you will find the end results differ depending on the material you use. Hemp is a wonderful material for creating bracelets and other jewelry designs. It is natural, durable, and holds its shape incredibly well. While embroidery floss is great for small, intricate designs or bracelets with lots of flexibility, hemp is perfect for larger, chunkier designs that will stay in place where you put them. Hemp is also an excellent material for first-time knotters. Because hemp is thicker and stiffer than embroidery floss, knots made in hemp are easy to follow, so correcting mistakes is simple.

Embroidery floss is also popular because of the wide range of colors available. But don't let color choice keep you from working with hemp—hemp is not what it used to be! While it is still available in its natural tan, hemp can now be found in a variety of other bright, variegated, and metallic colors, so you will be sure to find something that fits your particular taste and style. (Go to page 16 to get a glimpse of some of the awesome hemp colors that are now on the market!)

So check out these designs and give hemp a try! Whether you're going for a boho chic look or trying to fuse retro with modern, you'll be sure to find something you love here.

Working with Hemp

To create a basic hemp design, the only things you'll need are hemp and scissors—it's that easy! You can make hemp designs as simple as you'd like with knotted closures, or as complex as you'd like with jewelry finding closures and bead embellishments. Here you'll find everything you need to know to start knotting with hemp.

MEASURING

Hemp projects are typically made up of working strands, which are used to tie the knots, and center (or filler) strands, around which the knots are tied. Because of this, working strands should be five to six times as long as the desired length of the finished piece if you intend to use close, dense knots, such as square knots. The more unknotted space or beads you plan to incorporate in your design, the shorter the working strands can be. If you knot tightly, you will likely use more cord, while if you knot loosely, you won't use as much. Just keep in mind that it's always better to have too much cord than too little! You can always make smaller projects like keychains from your leftovers.

For insurance, center strands should be about twice as long as the desired length of the finished piece, plus enough length to allow you to tie your ending knot easily. Again, too much is always better than too little!

GETTING STARTED

1 Measure and trim strands of hemp to the length you need.

2 Fold the strands in half to find and align the center points.

3 Tie an overhand knot at the folded end of the hemp to form a ½" (1.5cm) loop. Bring the working strands to the outside (left and right sides) of the piece before you begin knotting.

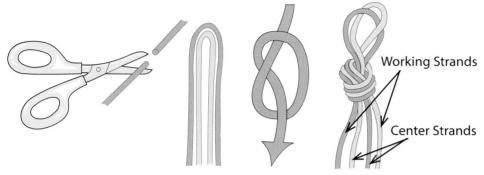

Working Strands

Center Strands

JEWELRY CLOSURES

Hemp projects are simple to finish with a loop on one end and a knot on the other (see the bracelet on page 20). For a more polished look, however, you can add jewelry closures.

To finish a project without tying knots, use fold-over crimps. Center the ends of the hemp strands on the fold-over crimp. Use pliers to fold each side of the crimp down over the hemp strands. Use jump rings to attach a clasp to the fold-over crimps. Be sure to twist the jumps rings open and closed so that they retain their shape. Do not pull the rings open.

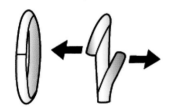

Twist your jump ring open, making sure you maintain the circular shape.

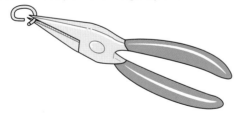

Do not pull the jump ring open from side to side so that it loses its shape.

Place the ends of your design in a fold-over crimp, and squeeze the crimp closed with pliers.

Use jump rings to attach a clasp to the fold-over crimps.

> **TIP**
> For extra-wide designs, use ribbon crimps instead of fold-over crimps. Ribbon crimps come in a variety of widths, so you can select the best fit for your project.

TIPS

Adding beads. Select beads with holes large enough to fit over the hemp strands you are using. Beads are typically threaded onto both center strands, although they can be added to just one center strand or to the outer working strands. If the holes in the beads you wish to use are too small, incorporate beading wire into your design so you can thread the beads onto the wire instead of the hemp (see below).

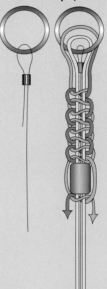

Use beading wire in your hemp designs to add beads with holes that are too small to be threaded directly onto the hemp.

Tightening knots. For strong knots, especially beginning and ending knots, tighten each strand individually. If possible, use pliers to pull strands tight for the ending knot.

Not enough cord. If you're running short on cord toward the end of your design, try switching the working strands with the center strands. Switching the strands will show a little, so hide the transition with a bead or in the middle of a knot if possible. Use glue as needed.

CREATE WITH COLOR!

Hemp is not what it used to be! Manufacturers are now creating hemp in fun and unique colors that will totally change the way you think about this knotting material. Natural hemp is a wonderful go-to for creating bohemian-style pieces, but now you can branch out and experiment with earthy tones like coral, olive, and navy. For those seeking an urban-chic look, you will find metallics and sets of coordinating neutrals. If your style is fresh and fun, you'll love hemp in neons and jewel tones. Check your local craft store for all the fun options available to you!

THE PROJECTS

It's time to get started! Each project in this book is built around a fundamental knot. Find a knot you like, and then learn how to create projects using it. Try using different colors of hemp, unique beads, or other embellishments to customize each piece to match your own personal taste and style. Try natural hemp with turquoise accents for a boho chic look. Metallic hemp with high-gloss beads will give you an edgy, urban feel. For a totally modern take, try using neon colors.

OVERHAND KNOT

OVERHAND KNOT

Basic overhand knot

Overhand knot with a loop

Multi-Strand Overhand Knot Bracelet

MATERIALS
* Four 1½' (45cm) strands of hemp
* About 28 beads of your choice

1 Using an overhand knot, tie all four strands together at one end, 4" (10cm) from the end.

2 Take one of the four strands. Leave a space, and then tie an overhand knot. Thread a bead onto the strand. Tie an overhand knot immediately following the bead. Repeat until you have a beaded section about 6" (15cm) long. Repeat with all the strands.

3 Tie the four strands together after the beaded sections using an overhand knot. Trim the ends to about 4" (10cm) long.

4 You will have four tails at each end of the bracelet. Tie an overhand knot at the end of each one and use the tails to tie the bracelet onto your wrist.

THREE-STRAND BRAID

THREE-STRAND BRAID

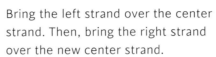

Bring the left strand over the center strand. Then, bring the right strand over the new center strand.

Repeat.

Beads and Braids Necklace

MATERIALS
* Six 5' (160cm) strands of hemp
* Seed beads in coordinating colors
* 3mm silver disk spacers

1. Align the ends of all six strands. Measure in 5" (10cm) from one end and tie all the strands together at the 5" (10cm) point using an overhand knot.

2. Divide the strands into three groups of two strands each. Braid the three groups together for 7" (18cm).

3. Divide the strands into two groups of three strands each. Tie an overhand knot in each group.

4. Thread beads and spacers onto all six strands using a random pattern. Bead for 8" (20cm) along each strand. When finished beading, braid or twist the beaded strands, or leave them untwisted.

5. Divide the strands into two groups of three strands each. Tie an overhand knot in each group.

6. Divide the strands into three groups of two strands each. Braid the three groups together for 7" (18cm).

7. Tie all six strands together at the end of the braid using an overhand knot. Trim the ends to 5" (10cm) long.

8. There will be six tails at each end of the necklace. Tie an overhand knot at the end of each one. Use the tails to tie on the necklace.

BASIC WRAP

BASIC WRAP

Place the strands to be wrapped together. Using one end of the wrapping strand, form a loop under the strands to be wrapped. Take the working end and begin wrapping it around the strands, working up toward the loop.

Continue tightly wrapping the strands until only a small portion of the original loop is visible. Thread the working end of the wrapping strand through the loop.

Gently pull on the starting end of the wrapping strand to bring the loop and the working end down into the wrap. Trim away the ends.

To add a closure, thread a bead or button onto the wrapping cord and position it at the top of the loop.

Simple Wrapped Bracelet

MATERIALS
* Two 1½' (45cm) strands of 2mm leather cord
* One 2' (60cm) strand of hemp
* Two 10" (25cm) strands of hemp
* Button for closure

1. Place the two leather cords side by side and measure in 9" (25cm) from one end.

2. Starting at the 9" (25cm) point, follow the diagrams above to form a wrap over the two cords with the 2' (60cm) piece of hemp. Wrap for 2" (5cm). Trim the ends.

3. Fold the leather cords in half at the center point of the wrap. Using one of the 10" (25cm) hemp strands, make another wrap about 1" (2.5cm) long over all four cords, directly after the first wrap.

4. Gather the four leather cords together at the opposite end of the bracelet. Thread a button onto the remaining 10" (25cm) piece of hemp and use it to form a 1" (2.5cm) wrap over the cord ends, using the button as a closure (see above).

5. Trim the hemp ends and dot with glue.

BASIC WEAVE

BASIC WEAVE

Six-strand woven band

Beaded Woven Bracelet

MATERIALS
* Three 2' (60cm) strands of hemp
* One 7½' (230cm) strand of hemp
* About forty-five to fifty 3mm tube beads

1 Tie an overhand knot (see 20) at one end of the 7½' (230cm) strand. Fold the three 2' (60cm) strands in half to form a loop at their center points.

2 Tie the three 2' (60cm) strands together at their center points, tying them over the knotted end of the 7½' (230cm) strand using an overhand knot with a ½" (1.5cm) loop at the top (see 20).

3 Divide the short 2' (60cm) strands into three groups of two strands each. Bring the long 7½' (230cm) strand through the filler strands as illustrated above, going over the first group, under the second group, over the third group, under the third group, over the second group, under the first group, and repeating.

4 Weave three rows through the short strands with the long strand. Then thread a bead onto the long strand and position it over the center group of short strands when you make your next pass. Weave another row without a bead.

5 Continue adding a bead on every other row as directed in Step 4 until all of the beads have been added or the bracelet reaches the desired length. Weave three rows without beads, and then tie all the strands together in an overhand knot. Trim the ends.

HALF HITCH KNOT

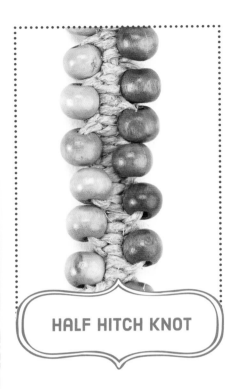

HALF HITCH KNOT

Left half hitch

Repeating left
half hitch

Right half hitch

Two-Color Twist Bracelet

MATERIALS
* Two 6' (180cm) strands of hemp (two colors)

1 Fold the two strands in half to find the center points. Tie the strands together at their center points using an overhand knot with a ½" (1.5cm) loop at the top.

2 Take a strand in the first color and use it to tie half hitches over all the other strands for 1" (2.5cm).

3 Take a strand in the second color and use it to tie half hitches over all the other strands for 1" (2.5cm).

4 Repeat Steps 2 and 3 until the bracelet reaches the desired length.

5 Tie all the strands together in an overhand knot. Trim the ends.

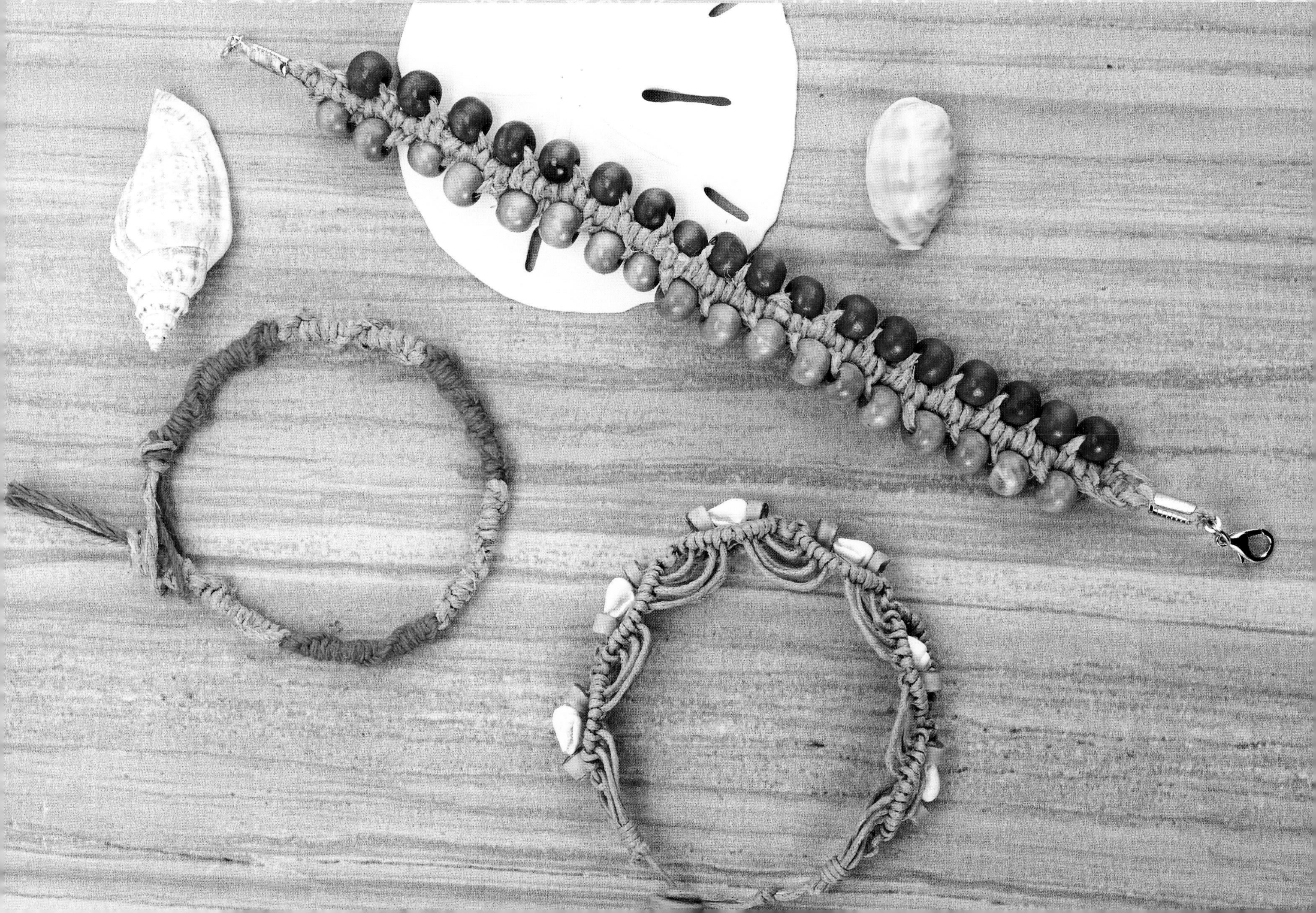

Beaded Half Hitch Bracelet

MATERIALS

* One 10' (300cm) strand of hemp
* One 1½' (45cm) strand of hemp
* Thirty-six 5mm round beads (two colors)
* 2 fold-over crimps
* 2 jump rings
* 1 clasp

1 Fold both hemp strands in half to find the center points. Hold the two strands together and attach a fold-over crimp over their center points.

2 Using the long left strand, tie two left half hitch knots (see page 28) over the two short strands. Using the long right strand, tie two right half hitch knots (see page 28) over the two short strands.

3 String a bead onto the long left strand and tie two left half hitch knots. String a bead onto the long right strand and tie two right half hitch knots.

4 Repeat Step 3 until all the beads have been added, alternating colors as desired. Then repeat Step 2.

5 Gather all the cords together at the end of the bracelet and attach a fold-over crimp. Use the jump rings to attach the clasp to the ends of the bracelet.

Shell Bracelet

MATERIALS

* Three 2½' (75cm) strands of hemp
* One 4' (120cm) strand of hemp
* One 2' (60cm) strand of hemp (beading strand)
* Twelve 3mm tube beads
* 6 shell beads
* One 10mm disk bead

Forward knot

Tie the left strand onto the right strand using a left half hitch knot.

Repeat, tying a second half hitch using the same strand.

Note that the strands have now switched places. The outer left strand has moved "forward" to the right.

Backward knot

Tie the right strand onto the left strand using a right half hitch knot.

Repeat, tying a second half hitch using the same strand.

Note that the strands have now switched places. The outer right strand has moved "backward" to the left.

1. Fold the 4' (120cm) strand in half to find the center point. Tie an overhand knot with a ½" (1.5cm) loop at the center point of the strand.

2. Measure ½" (1.5cm) from the overhand knot. Place one end of the 2' (60cm) beading strand at this point. Fold the 2½' (75cm) strands in half to find their center points. Tie the 2½' (75cm) strands onto the 4' (120cm) strand and the 2' (60cm) beading strand at the ½" (1.5cm) point using an overhand knot.

3. You will have six short strands, one beading strand, and two long strands. We will call the long strands filler strands and the short strands working strands. Position the beading strand in the center. Using the two long filler strands, tie two square knots (see 44) over the beading strand.

4. Take the third from left working strand and use it to tie a forward knot (see above) on the left filler strand. Repeat with the second from left and outer left working strands. This will move the filler strand to the left side of the bracelet.

5. Repeat Step 4 with the three right working strands, using backward knots (see above) to tie them onto the right filler strand. This will move the filler strand to the right side of the bracelet.

6. Take the first left working strand and use it to tie a backward knot on the left filler strand. Repeat with the second from left and third from left working strands. This will move the filler strand back to the center of the bracelet.

7. Repeat Step 6 with the three right working strands, using forward knots to tie them onto the right filler strand. This will move the filler strand back to the center of the bracelet.

8. Thread a tube bead, a shell bead, and then a second tube bead onto the beading strand. Then use the filler strands to tie a square knot over the beading strand after the last bead.

9. Repeat Steps 4–8 until all the beads have been added. When finished, you will have six beaded sections.

10. Use the filler strands to tie one more square knot over the beading strand. Then, tie all the strands together in an overhand knot.

11. Trim away all the strands except the beading strand. Thread the disk bead onto the beading strand and tie an overhand knot after the bead, ½" (1.5cm) from the overhand knot you tied in Step 10.

JOSEPHINE KNOT

JOSEPHINE KNOT

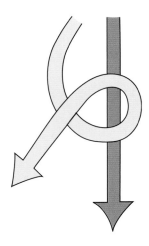

Use the left working strand to form a loop on top of the right working strand.

Bring the working end of the right strand over the working end of the left strand.

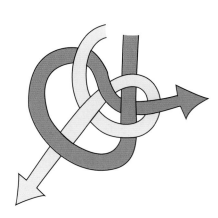

Feed the working end of the right strand through the knot as shown, following an alternating under-over pattern.

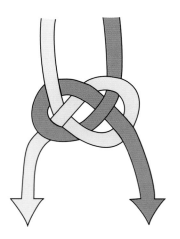

Pull on the starting and working ends of both strands to close and shape the knot.

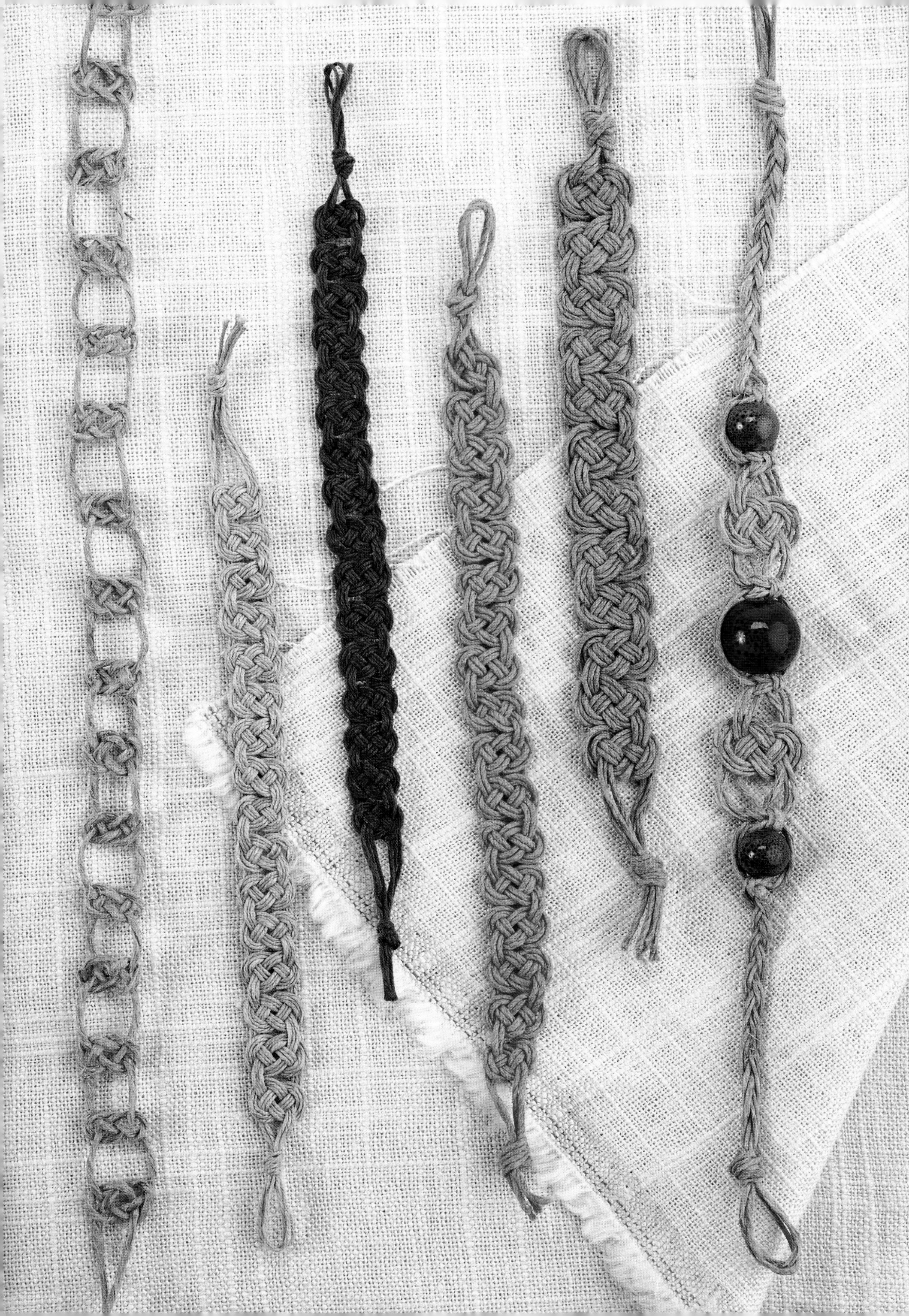

Josephine Knot Necklace

MATERIALS
* One 7½' (230cm) strand of hemp

1 Fold the strand in half to form a loop at the center. Tie an overhand knot with a ½" (1.5cm) loop at the center point.

2 Leave ½" (1.5cm) of space and follow the illustrations on page 32 to tie a Josephine knot. You can leave the knot loose, so there is a lot of space between the strands, or tighten it, so the knot is small and dense.

3 Leave ½" (1.5cm) of space and tie another Josephine knot. Continue until the necklace reaches the desired length.

4 Finish with an overhand knot. Trim the ends.

Multi-Strand Josephine Knot Bracelet

MATERIALS
* Two or three 12½' (380cm) strands of hemp

TIP
For even more wow factor, make a two-color bracelet. Use three strands, two in one color and one in a coordinating color. Put the two strands of the same color on either side of the second color when tying the knot.

1 Fold the strands in half to form a loop at the center points. Tie the strands together at their center points using an overhand knot with a ½" (1.5cm) loop at the top.

2 Divide the strands into two evenly sized groups. Follow the illustrations on page 32 to tie a Josephine knot, treating each group of strands as one. Keep the strands in each group parallel as you form the knot.

3 Continue tying Josephine knots until the bracelet reaches the desired length. You can tie the knots close together for a dense, chunky design, or you can space them out for a more airy look.

4 Finish with an overhand knot. Trim the ends.

Beaded Josephine Knot Bracelet

MATERIALS
* Three 4½' (140cm) strands of hemp
* One 15mm round focal bead
* Two 10mm round beads

35

> **TIP**
> To make this bracelet longer or shorter, adjust the length of the braids at each end.

1 Fold the strands in half to form a loop at the center points. Tie the strands together at their center points using an overhand knot with a ½" (1.5cm) loop at the top.

2 Divide the strands into three groups of two strands each. Braid the three groups together (see page 22) for 1½" (4cm).

3 Use the two outer strand groups to tie a square knot (see 44) over the inner strand group. Thread one of the 10mm round beads onto both inner strands. Use the outer groups to tie a square knot immediately following the bead.

4 Divide the strands into two groups of three strands each. Leave about ¼" (0.5cm) of space after the square knot and tie a Josephine knot.

5 Divide the strands into three groups of two strands each. Leave about ½" (1.5cm) of space and use the outer groups to tie a square knot over the inner group. Thread the focal bead onto both inner strands. Use the outer groups to tie a square knot immediately following the bead.

6 Repeat Step 4. Then divide the strands into three groups of two strands each. Leave about ¼" (0.5cm) of space and use the outer groups to tie a square knot over the inner group. Thread a 10mm round bead onto both inner strands. Use the outer groups to tie a square knot immediately following the bead.

7 Braid the three groups together for 1½" (4cm). Finish with an overhand knot. Trim the ends.

HALF KNOT TWIST

HALF KNOT TWIST

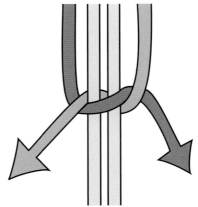

Bring the right working strand under the center strands and over the left working strand. Bring the left working strand over the center strands and under the right working strand.

Repeat, always bringing the right strand under the center strands and over the left strand, and always bringing the left strand over the center strands and under the right strand.

Tying the half knot will naturally cause the working strands to twist around the center strands as you go, forming a spiral shape.

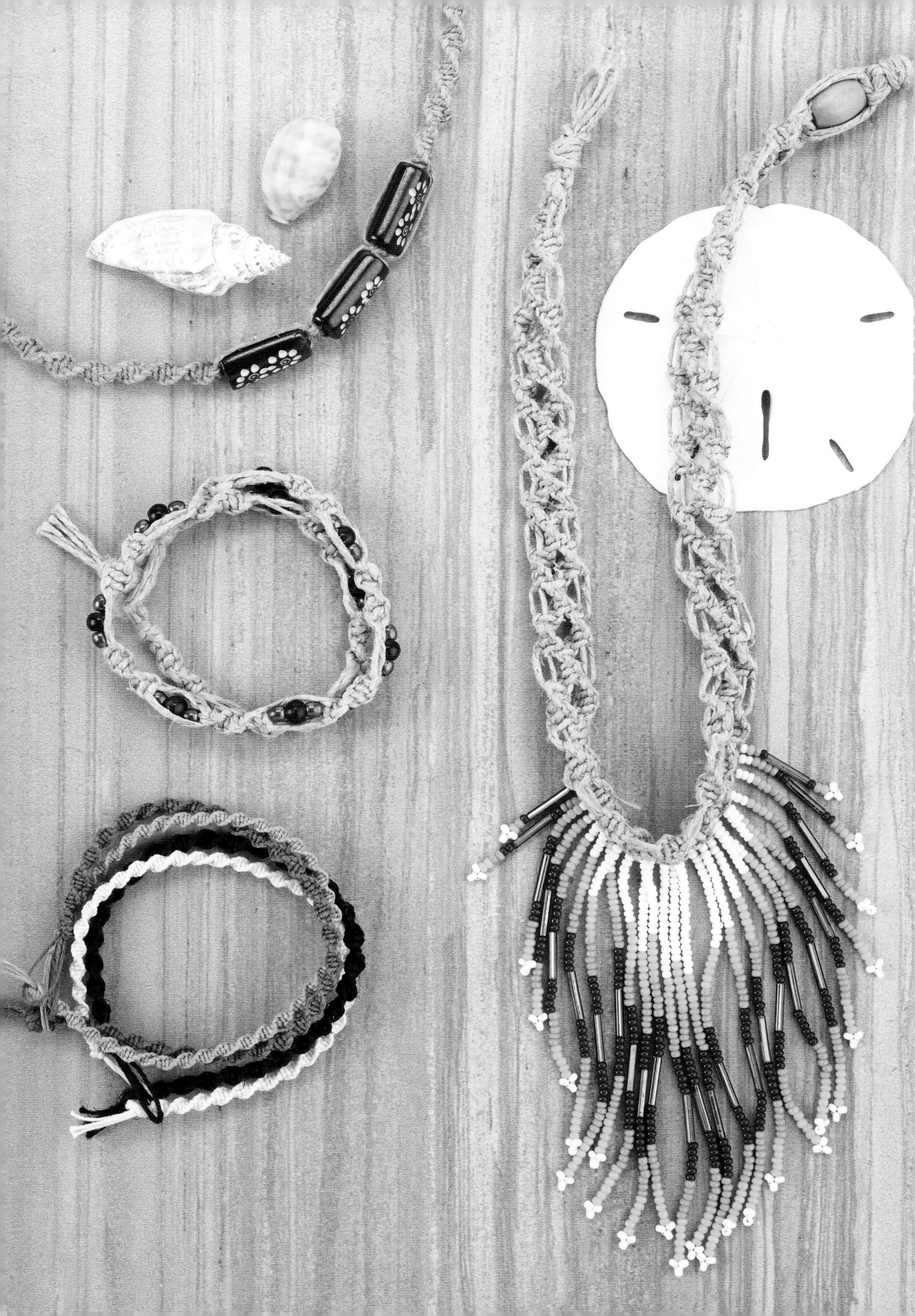

Simple Half Knot Bracelet

MATERIALS
* One 2' (60cm) strand of hemp
* One 6' (180cm) strand of hemp

1 Fold the strands in half to form a loop at the center points. Tie the strands together at their center points using an overhand knot with a ½" (1.5cm) loop at the top.

2 Follow the illustrations on page 36 to tie half knots around the short center strands with the long working strands until the bracelet reaches the desired length.

3 Finish with an overhand knot.

Two-Color Half Knot Bracelet

MATERIALS
* Two 6' (180cm) strands of hemp (two colors)

1 Fold the strands in half to form a loop at the center. Tie the strands together at their center points using an overhand knot with a ½" (1.5cm) loop at the top.

2 Take the two strands of Color 1 and use them to tie half knots around the two strands of Color 2. Continue for about 1" (2.5cm).

3 Switch colors, bringing the Color 2 strands to the outside of the bracelet. Use the Color 2 strands to tie half knots around the two strands of Color 1. Continue for about 1" (2.5cm).

4 Continue tying half knots until the bracelet reaches the desired length, switching colors every 1" (2.5cm). Finish with an overhand knot.

Bold Bead Necklace

MATERIALS

* One 2½' (75cm) strand of hemp
* One 10' (300cm) strand of hemp
* Three 20mm tube beads
* 2 fold-over crimps
* 2 jump rings
* 1 clasp

1 Fold both hemp strands in half to find the center points. Hold the two strands together and attach a fold-over crimp over their center points.

2 Follow the illustrations on page 36 to tie half knots around the short center strands with the long working strands for 6" (15cm).

3 Thread a bead onto the two center strands, and then tie a square knot (page 44) after it to hold it in place. Repeat with a second bead. Thread the remaining bead onto the two center strands. Do not tie a square knot after it.

4 Tie half knots after the last bead for 6" (15cm).

5 Gather all the strands together at the end of the necklace and attach a fold-over crimp. Use the jump rings to attach the clasp to the ends of the necklace.

TIP

To make this necklace longer or shorter, adjust the length of the knotted section on either side of the beaded section.

Beaded Twist Necklace

MATERIALS
* One 2½' (75cm) strand of hemp
* One 5' (150cm) strand of hemp
* Eleven 5mm round beads
* Twenty-two 3mm round beads

TIP

To make this necklace longer or shorter, adjust the length of the knotted section on either side of the necklace.

1 Fold the strands in half to form a loop at the center points. Tie the strands together at their center points using an overhand knot with a ½" (1.5cm) loop at the top.

2 Tie half knots around the short center strands with the long working strands for about 1" (2.5cm).

3 Thread a 3mm bead, a 5mm bead, and then a second 3mm bead onto one of the center strands. Tie half knots after the last bead added for ½" (1.5cm).

4 Repeat Step 3 until all of the beads have been added. After the final bead, tie half knots for 1" (2.5cm) instead of ½" (1.5cm). Finish with an overhand knot.

Fringed Necklace

1 Fold the strands in half to form a loop at the center points. Tie the strands together at their center points using an overhand knot with a ½" (1.5cm) loop at the top.

2 Separate the strands into two groups of four strands each. Tie six half knots with each group of strands (page 36).

3 Use the four center strands to tie six half knots.

4 Repeat Steps 2–3 to tie an alternating half knot twist pattern (see below) for 1 ½' (45cm) or until the choker reaches the desired length.

5 Thread the oval bead onto the two center strands. Use the remaining strands on each side of the center strands as one to tie two half knots over the center strands, immediately following the bead.

6 Tie all the strands together in an overhand knot. Dot with glue and trim the ends.

7 Use the beading needle and thread to attach the seed bead fringe to the center of the necklace. Thread the beads according to illustration below left. Create the individual strands according to the list below.

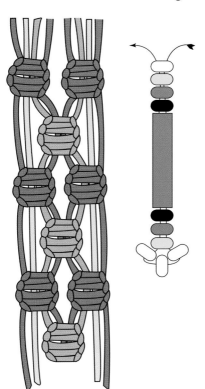

Strand 1: 1W, 1Y, 1T, 1B, bugle, 1B, 1T, 1Y, 3W
Strand 2: 2W, 2Y, 2T, 2B, bugle, 2B, 2T, 2Y, 3W
Strand 3: 3W, 3Y, 3T, 3B, bugle, 3B, 3T, 3Y, 3W
Strand 4: 4W, 4Y, 4T, 4B, bugle, 4B, 4T, 4Y, 3W
Strand 5: 5W, 5Y, 5T, 5B, bugle, 5B, 5T, 5Y, 3W
Strand 6: 6W, 6Y, 6T, 6B, bugle, 6B, 6T, 6Y, 3W
Strand 7: 8W, 6Y, 6T, 6B, bugle, 6B, 6T, 6Y, 3W
Strand 8: 10W, 6Y, 6T, 6B, bugle, 6B, 6T, 6Y, 3W
Strand 9: 12W, 6Y, 6T, 6B, bugle, 6B, 6T, 6Y, 3W
Strand 10: 14W, 6Y, 6T, 6B, bugle, 6B, 6T, 6Y, 3W
Strand 11: 16W, 6Y, 6T, 6B, bugle, 6B, 6T, 6Y, 3W
Strand 12: 18W, 6Y, 6T, 6B, bugle, 6B, 6T, 6Y, 3W
Strand 13: 20W, 6Y, 6T, 6B, bugle, 6B, 6T, 6Y, 3W
Strands 14–25: Repeat Strands 1–12 in reverse order.

MATERIALS
* Four 10' (300cm) strands of hemp
* About 300 white seed beads
* About 250 yellow seed beads
* About 250 turquoise seed beads
* About 250 brown seed beads
* Twenty-five 13mm bugle beads
* One 13mm oval bead for closure
* Beading needle and thread

FRINGE
W = White
Y = Yellow
T = Turquoise
B = Brown

HALF KNOT AND SQUARE KNOT

HALF KNOT AND
SQUARE KNOT

Lark's head knot

Watchband

MATERIALS
* Four 6' (180cm) strands of hemp
* Three 6" (15cm) strands of hemp
* Four 6mm round beads
* Watch face with bars
* Watch buckle

1 Fold the 6' (180cm) strands in half to form a loop at the center points. Tie the strands to the watch buckle at their center points using lark's head knots. Tie two on each side of the buckle tine.

2 Use the two outer left strands and the two outer right strands as one, tie five square knots (page 44) over the four center strands.

3 Separate the strands into two groups of four strands each. Use the outer cords in each group to tie a square knot over the two center cords.

4 Using the outer three strands from each group, tie six half knots (page 36). Thread both inner loose strands through a bead.

5 Repeat Steps 3 and 4 twice more to tie a square knot and six half knot twists with each group of strands. Thread both inner loose strands through a bead as before. After you have added the third bead, repeat Step 3.

6 Thread the watch face onto the strands by feeding the strands between the bar and the watch face on one side, under the watch face, and then between the bar and the watch face on the other side.

7 Repeat Steps 3–5 to begin tying the other side of the watchband. Repeat Step 2 to finish the other side of the watchband. To make the band longer, tie more square knots; to make the band shorter, tie fewer square knots.

8 Pull the last knot very tight. Trim the strands and generously cover the ends with glue to secure the knot.

SQUARE KNOT

SQUARE KNOT

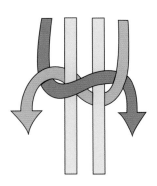

Bring the right working strand under the center strands and over the left working strand. Bring the left working strand over the center strands and under the right working strand.

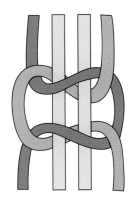

Bring the right working strand over the center strands and under the left working strand. Bring the left working strand under the center strands and over the right working strand.

Basic Square Knot Bracelet

MATERIALS
* Two 6' (180cm) strands of hemp (one or two colors)

TIP
Finish this project with jewelry closures by replacing the overhand knots at each end of the bracelet with fold-over crimps. Use jump rings to attach a clasp to the crimps.

1 Fold the two strands in half to form a loop at the center points.

2 Arrange the strands to create the color pattern you desire. To create a dual-color bracelet, make sure the outermost strands are two different colors. Tie the strands together at their center points using an overhand knot with a ½" (1.5cm) loop at the top.

3 Use the outer strands to tie square knots (see above) over the center strands. If creating a two-color bracelet, remember the strands that cross over the center strands will appear at the center of the finished bracelet; the strands that cross under the center strands will appear at the outside of the finished bracelet.

4 Continue tying square knots until the bracelet reaches the desired length. Finish with an overhand knot.

Pendant Necklace

MATERIALS
* Two 9' (275cm) strands of hemp
* Two 5' (150cm) strands of hemp
* 1 focal pendant

TIP
For the peace sign pendant used in this project, the strands were simply threaded through the spaces on either side of the top vertical bar. Lark's head knots can be used to attach pendants with a ring shape. If your pendant does not have a large space for you to thread your hemp through, attach a jump ring to the pendant and thread the hemp through it.

1 Fold all four strands in half to form a loop at the center points. Tie the strands to the pendant at their center points using lark's head knots. (see page xx) See the tip above for attaching different types of pendants.

2 Take two of the long strands and use them to tie two square knots over the remaining strands.

3 Separate the strands into two groups of four strands each. Make sure each group has two long strands and two short strands. Use the long strands in each group to tie square knots over the short strands for 2½" (6.5cm).

4 Working with one group at a time, leave about ¾" (2cm) of space. Switch the outer strands with the center strands and use the new outer strands to tie a square knot over the new center strands. Repeat for about 7" (18cm). Do this with both groups.

5 In each group, tie an overhand knot after the last square knot. There will be four tails at each end of the necklace. Trim them to about 7" (18cm) long and tie an overhand knot near the end of each one. Use the tails to tie on the necklace.

Simple Beaded Necklace

MATERIALS
* Three 5' (150cm) strands of hemp
* One 6mm disk bead
* Two 3mm round beads
* Five 6mm focal beads

TIP
To make this necklace longer or shorter, adjust the length of the braided sections on either side of the necklace.

1 Tie the strands together at one end using an overhand knot. Leave a 1" (2.5cm) space and tie a second overhand knot with all three strands. Repeat until you have tied seven overhand knots (including the starting knot).

2 Braid the three strands together for 7" (18cm). Then, tie an overhand knot with all three strands. Use the two outer strands to tie a square knot over the center strand.

3 Thread a 3mm bead onto the center strand. Use the two outer strands to tie a square knot after the 3mm bead.

4 Thread a 6mm focal bead onto the center strand. Use the two outer strands to tie a square knot after the 6mm bead. Repeat until all five beads have been added.

5 Repeat Step 3 to add the remaining 3mm bead. Then tie an overhand knot with all three strands.

6 Braid the three strands together for 7" (18cm). Tie an overhand knot with all three strands. Thread the disk bead onto all three strands. Tie an overhand knot after the bead and trim the ends.

Two-Color Chain Necklace

MATERIALS

* Two 8½' (260cm) strands of hemp (two colors)
* 4mm ball chain necklace, 1½' (45cm) long

1 Fold the Color 1 strand in half to form a loop at the center point. Center the Color 1 strand under the chain necklace, after the first ball in the chain.

2 Use the Color 1 strand to tie a square knot (see 44) over the chain necklace, between the first and second balls in the chain.

3 Repeat Steps 1–2 to tie the Color 2 strand onto the chain necklace, between the second and third balls in the chain.

4 Use the Color 1 strands to tie a square knot after the third ball in the chain. Use the Color 2 strands to tie a square knot after the fourth ball in the chain.

5 Repeat Step 4, tying square knots in alternating colors the length of the chain.

6 To finish, tie a final square knot with each color. Trim the ends as close to the finishing knots as possible and dot with glue.

Flower Necklace

MATERIALS
* Four 4' (120cm) strands of hemp
* Three 5mm round beads
* Eighteen 3mm round beads
* One 5mm disk bead

1. Tie the four strands together at one end with an overhand knot.

2. Thread the disk bead onto all four strands. Tie an overhand knot after the bead using all four strands.

3. Use the outer strands to tie square knots (see 44) over the center strands for 1" (2.5cm).

4. Leave 1" (2.5cm) of space. Switch the outer strands with the center strands. Use the new outer strands to tie two square knots over the new center strands. Repeat two more times, switching the outer and center strands each time before tying the square knots.

5. Thread three 3mm beads onto each of the outer strands. Thread a 5mm bead onto both center strands. Using the outer strands, tie two square knots after all the beads. This forms the first flower.

6. Leave 1" (2.5cm) of space. Switch the outer strands with the center strands and use the new outer strands to tie two square knots over the new center strands. Then repeat Step 5 to form the second flower. Repeat once more to form the third flower.

7. Leave 1" (2.5cm) of space. Switch the outer strands with the center strands and use the new outer strands to tie two square knots over the new center strands. Repeat one more time.

8. Leave 1" (2.5cm) of space. Switch the outer strands with the center strands and use the new outer strands to tie square knots for 1" (2.5cm). Use all the strands to tie an overhand knot after the square knots. Trim away two of the strands and dot the knot with glue.

9. Leave ½" (1.5cm) of space and then tie an overhand knot with the two remaining strands. Repeat five more times for six overhand knots total. Trim away any excess after the final overhand knot.

Double Bead Necklace

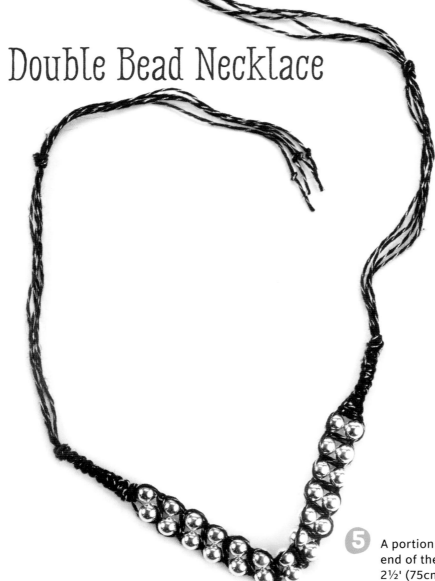

MATERIALS
- Three 4' (120cm) strands of hemp
- Two 2½' (75cm) strands of hemp
- Two 7" (18cm) pieces of beading wire
- Twenty-six 6mm round beads
- 4 crimp tubes
- Crimping pliers

1 Thread thirteen beads onto each piece of beading wire. Use the crimping pliers to attach a crimp tube before the first bead and after the last bead on each wire so the beads are held in place at the center of the wires.

2 Place the two beaded wire pieces side by side. Fold a 4' (120cm) strand of hemp in half to form a loop at the center point. Tie the strand onto the beaded wires at its center point, before the first set of beads, using an overhand knot.

3 Use the attached strand to tie a square knot (see 44) over the wire pieces, between the first and second set of beads.

4 Repeat Step 3 until square knots have been tied around all the bead sets on the wire pieces. After the last square knot has been tied, trim the ends and dot with glue.

5 A portion of wire should remain exposed at each end of the necklace. Fold a 4' (120cm) and a 2½' (75cm) strand in half to form a loop at the center points. Tie the strands onto the wire ends at one end of the necklace at their center points using an overhand knot. Tie the strands over the crimp tubes so they are right up against the beaded portion of the necklace.

6 Use the long strands to tie square knots over the wire ends and short strands. When the wire pieces end, continue tying knots over the short strands. Knot for about 1½" (4cm).

7 Tie an overhand knot with all four strands after the last square knot. Measure about 5" (12.5cm) from the overhand knot and tie a second overhand knot. Trim the ends to about 5" (12.5cm) long and tie an overhand knot at the end of each one.

8 Repeat Steps 5–7 to finish the other end of the necklace. The center beaded portion of the necklace can be gently shaped as desired.

Elegant Beaded Necklace

MATERIALS

* One 6½' (200cm) strand of hemp
* Two 5' (150cm) strands of hemp
* One 6mm pony bead
* 1 seed bead for closure
* 64 blue seed beads
* 48 green seed beads

1 Fold the 6½' (200cm) strand in half to form a loop at the center point. Tie the strand at its center point using an overhand knot with a ½" (1.5cm) loop at the top.

2 Measure in ½" (1.5cm) from the overhand knot and tie a second overhand knot using both strands. Repeat this twice more for four overhand knots total (including the starting knot).

3 Measure in 2" (5cm) from the last overhand knot. Find the center points of the two 5' (150cm) strands. Using an overhand knot, tie the 5' (150cm) strands onto the 6½' (200cm) strand at the 2" (5cm) point.

4 Use the two outer strands to tie three square knots over the four center strands.

5 Thread a blue seed bead onto each outer strand. Then use the outer strands to tie four square knots over the four center strands. Repeat this three more times (you will add eight beads total). On the last repeat, only tie two square knots after the beads instead of four.

6 Thread five green beads onto the outer left strand. Thread three blue beads onto the second strand from the left. Thread five blue beads onto the outer right strand. Thread three green beads onto the second strand from the right. Leave the two center strands loose.

7 Tie a square knot with the four center strands. Then, separate the strands into two groups of three strands each. Use the outer strands in each group to tie a square knot.

8 Repeat Steps 6–7, threading beads onto the strands as follows: six blue on outer left, four green on second from left, six green on outer right, four blue on second from right.

9 Repeat Steps 6–7, threading beads onto the strands as follows: seven green on outer left, five blue on second from left, seven blue on outer right, five green on second from right.

10 Repeat Step 8, following the beading instructions exactly. Then Repeat Step 6, following the beading instructions exactly. When finished, your necklace will have five beaded sections.

11 Use the two outer strands to tie two square knots over the four center strands after the last beaded section.

12 Thread a blue seed bead onto each outer strand. Then use the outer strands to tie four square knots over the four center strands. Repeat this three more times (you will add eight beads total). On the last repeat, only tie three square knots after the beads instead of four.

13 Tie all the strands together in an overhand knot. Trim away three of the strands. Measure 2" (5cm) from the overhand knot and tie the three strands together in an overhand knot. Trim away two of the strands. Thread the pony bead and a seed bead onto the final strand. Tie an overhand knot and trim the end.

ALTERNATING SQUARE KNOT

ALTERNATING SQUARE KNOT

Four-strand alternating square knot pattern

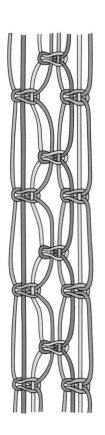

Eight-strand alternating square knot pattern

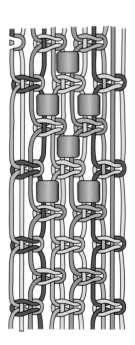

Twelve-strand alternating square knot pattern, plus beads

Simple Choker

MATERIALS
* Two 6½' (200cm) strands of hemp
* 2 fold-over crimps
* 2 jump rings
* 1 clasp

1 Fold both hemp strands in half to find the center points. Hold the two strands together and attach a fold-over crimp over their center points.

2 Knot the choker using a four-strand alternating square knot pattern (see 52). Knot until the choker reaches the desired length.

3 Gather all the strands together at the end of the choker and attach a fold-over crimp. Use the jump rings to attach the clasp to the ends of the choker.

54

Beaded Cuff Bracelet

MATERIALS
* Four 4½' (140cm) strands of hemp
* Three 15mm tube beads

1 Fold the four strands in half to form a loop at the center. Tie the strands together at their center points using an overhand knot with a ½" (1.5cm) loop at the top.

2 Tie an eight-strand alternating square knot pattern (see 52) for six rows. Thread a bead onto the two center strands.

3 Continue the alternating square knot pattern for three rows. Thread a bead onto the two center strands. Repeat once more to add the third bead.

4 After the third bead, continue the alternating square knot pattern for six rows. Tie all the strands together in an overhand knot and trim the ends.

Bold Beaded Choker

MATERIALS
* Six 10½' (320cm) strands of hemp
* Three 25mm tube beads
* Fifty-eight 6mm tube beads

1. Fold the six strands in half to form a loop at the center points. Tie the strands together at their center points using an overhand knot with a ½" (1.5cm) loop at the top.

2. Tie a twelve-strand alternating square knot pattern (see 52) for three rows.

3. Thread the fourth and fifth strands from the left through the same 6mm bead. Repeat with the fourth and fifth strands from the right. When finished, you will have added two beads.

4. Skip the first two strands on the left side. Tie a square knot with the next four strands. Tie a square knot with the next four strands. Leave the remaining two strands on the right side loose.

5. Tie two square knots with the first four strands on the left. Repeat with the first four strands on the right. Thread a bead onto the two center strands. Tie a square knot with the four center strands.

6. Repeat Steps 3–5 until twenty-nine beads have been added. You will end on a repeat of Step 4.

7. Thread the second and third strands from the left through the same 25mm bead. Repeat with the second and third strands from the right. Repeat with the two center strands.

8. Repeat Step 4 to tie two square knots across the choker.

9. Repeat Steps 3–5 until twenty-nine beads have been added. You will end on a repeat of Step 4.

10. Tie a twelve-strand alternating square knot pattern (see 52) for two rows. Tie all the strands together in an overhand knot. Tie a second overhand knot ½" (1.5cm) from the first. Trim the ends.

BAG NECKLACES

STARTING A BAG

Lark's head knot variation

1 Center the strap cord on a knotting board. Use T-pins to pin the cord in place. Because the cord is so long, there will be a lot that extends off both sides of the board. Gather these long ends in to bundles and use rubber bands to hold them in place.

2 Take half of the knotting cords and find the center points. Mount these cords onto the strap cord using the variation on the lark's head knot shown above.

3 Turn the knotting board so the strap cord is positioned vertically and the knotting cords are positioned horizontally.

4 Center one of the decorative cords on top of the knotting cords, parallel to the strap cord. Pin the top end (the end farthest from you) of the decorative cord in place on the knotting board.

5 Starting with the top (farthest from you) knotting cord, tie each knotting cord onto the decorative cord using two half hitch knots (see at right). Pull the knots snug as you work so the decorative cord butts up against the strap cord.

Left half hitch

If your decorative strand is to the right of your strap strand, use this half hitch knot.

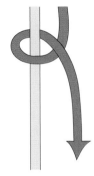

Right half hitch

If your decorative strand is to the left of your strap strand, use this half hitch knot.

KNOTTING THE FRONT

1 The bodies of most of the bags are tied using an alternating square knot pattern (see at right). Follow the individual instructions for your chosen bag design to tie the front of the bag.

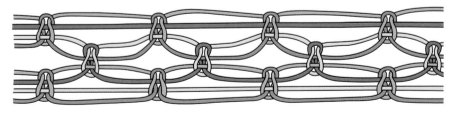

Alternating square knot pattern

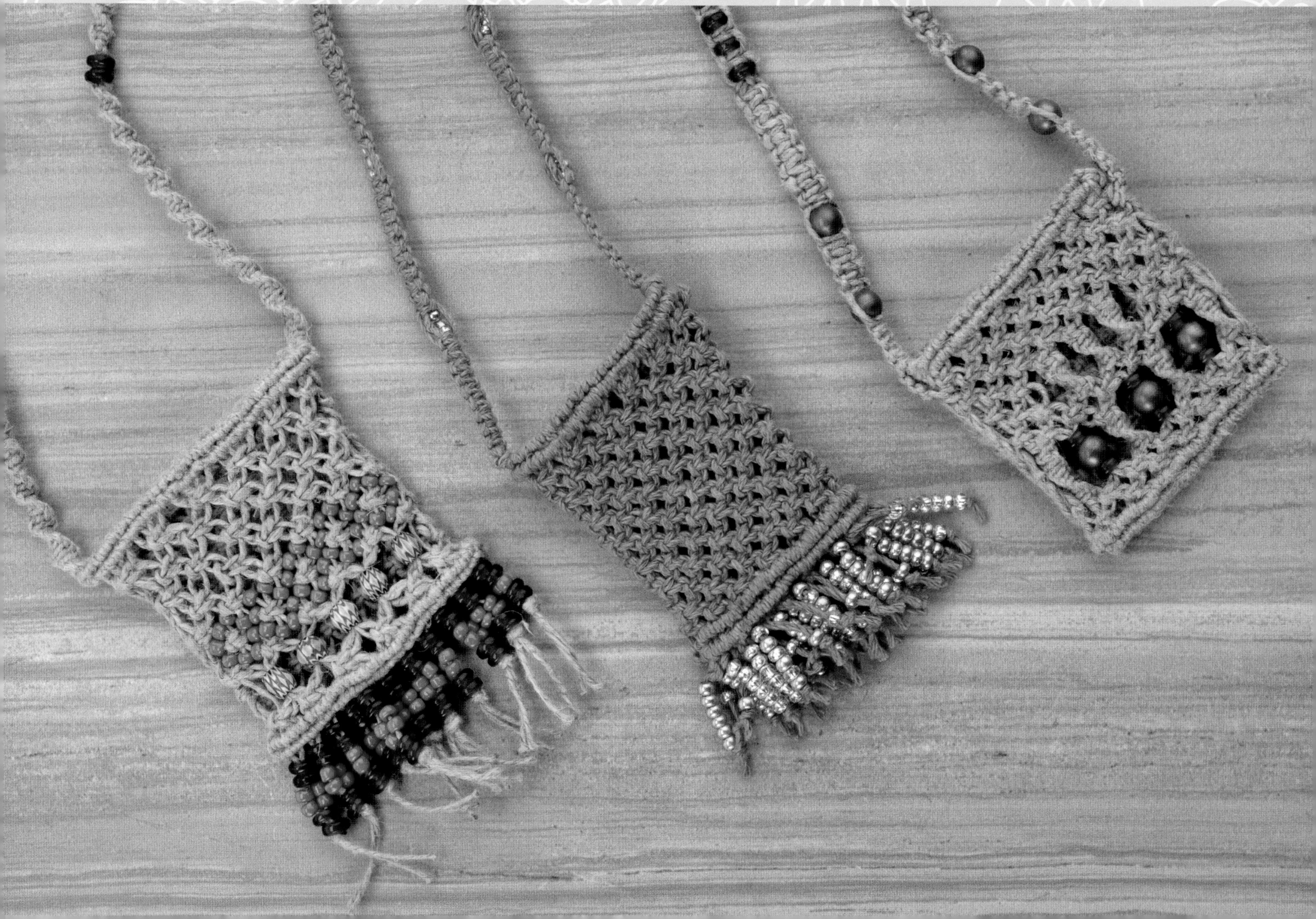

FINISHING THE BOTTOM

1 Turn the knotting board so the strap cord is positioned vertically and the knotting cords are positioned horizontally. Center one of the bottom cords on the knotting board, on top of the knotting cords and parallel to the strap cord. Pin the top end (the end farthest from you) of the bottom cord in place.

2 Starting with the top (farthest from you) knotting cord, tie each knotting cord onto the bottom cord using two half hitch knots (see 56). Pull the knots snug as you work so the bottom cord butts up against the body of the bag.

3 Turn the knotting board 180 degrees so the knotting cord you just tied onto the bottom cord is at the top (farthest from you). Fold the bottom cord back on itself so it is parallel with the bottom of the bag and on top of the knotting cords.

4 Starting with the top (farthest from you) knotting cord, tie each knotting cord onto the bottom cord using two half hitch knots (see 56) as before. Pull the knots snug as you work so the second row butts up against the first row you knotted in Step 2.

KNOTTING THE BACK

1 The back of the bag is created following the same steps used to make the front of the bag. Using the remaining strap and decorative cords, repeat the steps for starting a bag.

2 Follow the individual instructions for your chosen bag design to tie the back of the bag.

3 Using the remaining bottom cord, repeat the steps for finishing the bottom of the bag.

CREATING FRINGE

1 For a bag with fringe, leave the knotting cords hanging free from the bottom of the bag when you sew the sides together in Step 1 of finishing the bag at right. Tie a few of the knotting cords from the front of the bag together with a few of the knotting cords from the back of the bag across the bottom to close it.

2 Finish the fringe by adding beads, tying overhand knots at the end of each strand, or trimming the strand ends to various lengths. Make sure you do not trim or knot the tail ends of the bottom cord with the fringe. Leave these free for sewing the sides of the bag.

NO FRINGE

1 For a bag without fringe, place the front and back pieces of the bag on your workspace with the knotting cords facing one another. Position the pieces so the tail ends of the bottom cords are not on the same side of the bag.

2 Take a knotting cord from the front piece and tie it together with its corresponding knotting cord from the back piece. Repeat until all the knotting cords from the front and back pieces have been tied together. Make sure you do not knot the tail ends of the bottom cords. Leave these free to sew the sides of the bag closed.

3 Dot all of the knots with glue. When dry, trim all of the ends. Fold the front and back pieces up, enclosing the knots on the inside of the bag.

FINISHING

1 Use the tail ends of the bottom cords to sew the sides of the bag together. Knot the tail ends together on the inside of the bag. Trim the ends and dot with glue for extra security.

2 At each side of the bag, you will have four cords: the tail ends of the strap cords and the tail ends of the decorative cords. At each side of the bag, use the strap cords to tie three square knots over the decorative cords. Then, continue tying square knots or half knots until the bag straps reach the desired length.

3 You can choose to leave spaces between the strap knots or add beads or other embellishments as desired.

4 To finish each strap, use all the cords to tie an overhand knot immediately following the last knot. Trim the ends, leaving 4" (10cm)-long tails. Tie an overhand knot at the end of each tail. Use the tails to tie the bag around your neck.

Beaded Fringe Bag Necklace

MATERIALS
* Two 10' (300cm) strands of hemp (strap cords)
* Two 3½' (110cm) strands of hemp (decorative cords)
* Twenty-four 2' (60cm) strands of hemp (knotting cords)
* Two 1½' (45cm) strands of hemp (bottom cords)
* Approximately 400 seed beads (two colors)
* Additional beads as desired for the strap

1. Follow the instructions on page 56 to start the front piece of your bag.

2. Using the knotting cords, tie fourteen rows of an alternating square knot pattern (see 56).

3. Follow the instructions on page 58 to finish the bottom of the front piece.

4. Repeat Steps 1–3 to create the back piece of the bag.

5. Follow the instructions on page 58 to sew the sides of the bag closed. Leave the knotting cords hanging free from the bottom of the bag to form fringe.

6. Thread the seed beads onto the fringe pieces as desired, mixing and matching the colors. Tie an overhand knot after the seed beads to hold them in place. Trim the ends of the fringe pieces.

7. Follow the instructions on page 58 to knot the bag straps. Use a square knot for the straps. Add additional beads to the straps as desired.

Beaded Diamond Bag Necklace

MATERIALS

* Two 10' (300cm) strands of hemp (strap cords)
* Two 3½' (110cm) strands of hemp (decorative cords)
* Twenty-four 2' (60cm) strands of hemp (knotting cords)
* Two 1½' (45cm) strands of hemp (bottom cords)
* Five 5mm round beads
* 88 seed beads
* Forty-eight 5mm disk beads
* Additional beads as desired for the strap

1 Follow the instructions on page 56 to start the front piece of your bag.

2 Using the knotting cords, tie five rows of an alternating square knot pattern (see 56).

3 Thread a seed bead onto every cord except the first two cords on the left and the first two cords on the right. You will add twenty beads total. Tie another row following the alternating square knot pattern. Repeat once more so the added beads form a diamond pattern.

4 For the next row, thread a 5mm bead onto four cords at a time in place of tying a square knot. Repeat across the bag until all the beads have been added. Tie another row following the alternating square knot pattern.

5 Follow the instructions on page 58 to finish the bottom of the front piece.

6 Follow the instructions on page 58 to start the back of your bag.

7 Using the knotting cords, tie ten to fifteen rows following the alternating square knot pattern (tie the necessary number of rows to make the back of the bag as long as the front of the bag).

8 Follow the instructions on page 58 to finish the bottom of the back piece.

9 Follow the instructions on page 58 to sew the sides of the bag closed. Leave twenty-four knotting cords hanging free from the bottom of the bag to form fringe.

10 Take two fringe pieces and thread two disk beads onto both strands. Thread two seed beads onto each strand. Thread two disk beads onto both strands. Tie an overhand knot with both strands after the last disk bead. Repeat with the remaining fringe pieces. Trim the ends of the fringe pieces.

11 Follow the instructions on page 58 to knot the bag straps. Use half knots for the straps. Add additional beads to the straps as desired.

Extra Twist Bag Necklace

1 Follow the instructions on page 56 to start the front piece of your bag.

2 Using the knotting cords, tie four rows of an alternating square knot pattern (see 56).

3 Starting on the left side of the front piece, use the first eight strands to continue the alternating square knot pattern for three rows. Using the next four strands, tie about eight half knots (the half knot section should match the length of the alternating square knot rows tied along the left side).

4 Tie half knots as directed in Step 3 with the next two sets of four strands. Use the final eight strands on the right side of the front piece to tie the alternating square knot pattern for three rows.

5 Tie two rows of an alternating square knot pattern (see 56).

6 Starting on the left side of the front piece, use the first four strands to tie ten half knots (page 36). Thread a 6mm bead, an 8mm bead, and then a 6mm bead onto the next four strands. Repeat across the front of the bag. Then tie two rows of an alternating square knot pattern.

7 Follow the instructions on page 58 to finish the bottom of the front piece.

8 Follow the instructions on page 58 to start the back of your bag.

9 Using the knotting cords, tie ten to fifteen rows following the alternating square knot pattern (tie the necessary number of rows to make the back of the bag as long as the front of the bag).

10 Follow the instructions on page 58 to finish the bottom of the back piece.

11 Follow the instructions on page 58 to sew the sides of the bag closed. Leave the knotting cords hanging free from the bottom of the bag to form fringe if desired.

12 Follow the instructions on page 58 to knot the bag straps. Use square knots for the straps. Add additional beads to the straps as desired.

MATERIALS

* Two 10' (300cm) strands of hemp (strap cords)
* Two 3½' (110cm) strands of hemp (decorative cords)
* Twenty-eight 2' (60cm) strands of hemp (knotting cords)
* Two 1½' (45cm) strands of hemp (bottom cords)
* Three 8mm round beads
* Six 6mm disk beads
* Additional beads as desired for the strap

Clasp Bag Necklace

1. Follow the instructions on page 56 to start the front piece of your bag. Repeat Steps 4 and 5 by folding the decorative cord back on itself and tying a second row of half hitch knots along it with the knotting strands.

2. Starting on the left side of the front piece, thread a tube bead onto the first two knotting strands. Repeat across the front of the bag, adding twelve beads.

3. Using a 1½' (45cm) decorative cord, repeat Steps 4 and 5 on page 56 to tie two rows of half hitches with the knotting strands.

4. Tie three rows of an alternating square knot pattern (see 56).

5. Take the sixth cord from the left and the sixth cord from the right. Thread them through each end of the 25mm tube bead. When finished, the bead will have one cord going into and one cord coming out of each end.

6. Tie the fourth row following the alternating square knot pattern as usual. Incorporate the cords threaded through the bead as usual. Do not pull these cords too tight.

7. Tie four rows of an alternating square knot pattern (see 56).

8. Follow the instructions on page 58 to finish the bottom of the front piece.

9. Follow the instructions on page 58 to start the back of your bag. Tie two rows of decorative half hitches with the knotting cords as you did for the front of the bag.

10. Tie two rows of an alternating square knot pattern.

11. Using a 1½' (45cm) decorative cord, repeat Steps 4 and 5 on page 56 to tie two rows of half hitches with the knotting strands.

12. Using the knotting cords, tie five to ten rows following the alternating square knot pattern (tie the necessary number of rows to make the back of the bag as long as the front of the bag).

13. Follow the instructions on page 58 to finish the bottom of the back piece.

14. Fold a 2½' (75cm) clasp cord in half to find the center point. Locate the center square knot in the first row on the back of the bag. Anchor the clasp cord by threading the ends through the back of the bag on either side the center square knot, so the center point of the clasp cord is behind the square knot. Repeat with the second clasp cord.

15. Using the clasp cords, tie square knots (page 44) for about 3" (7cm). Using all four strands, tie two overhand knots, one on top of the other. Tie two more square knots, then tie two overhand knots on top of one another again. Trim the ends.

16. Follow the instructions on page 58 to sew the sides of the bag closed. Leave the knotting cords hanging free from the bottom of the bag to form fringe.

17. For the fringe, thread tube beads onto two strands at a time, selecting the strands randomly. Secure the beads by tying overhand knots after them. Trim the ends of the fringe pieces even.

18. Follow the instructions on page 58 to knot the bag straps. Use square knots for the straps. Add additional beads to the straps as desired.

MATERIALS

* Two 10' (300cm) strands of hemp (strap cords)
* Two 3½' (110cm) strands of hemp (decorative cords)
* Two 1½' (45cm) strands of hemp (decorative cords)
* Twenty-four 2' (60cm) strands of hemp (knotting cords)
* Two 1½' (45cm) strands of hemp (bottom cords)
* Two 2½' (75cm) strands of hemp (clasp cords)
* Forty 10mm tube beads
* One 25mm tube bead
* Additional beads as desired for the strap

KNOT INDEX

OVERHAND KNOT 20

OVERHAND KNOT WITH LOOP 20

THREE-STRAND BRAID 22

BASIC WRAP 24

BASIC WEAVE 26

HALF HITCH KNOT 28

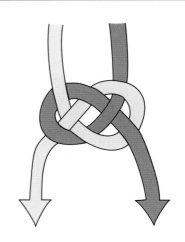

JOSEPHINE KNOT 32

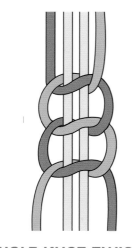

HALF KNOT TWIST 36

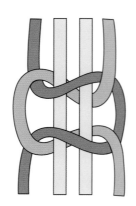

SQUARE KNOT 44

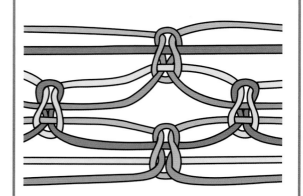

ALTERNATING SQUARE KNOT 52